Messages From a Boy with an Absentee Father

DIVINE WORDSMITH

Illustrations by: Dillon Wright

MESSAGES FROM A BOY WITH AN ABSENTEE FATHER

Copyright © 2023 Divine Wordsmith

All rights reserved. No part of this publication may be reproduced, distributed, stored in a retrieval system or transmitted, recording, or other electronic or mechanical methods, without the prior written permission of the author, except by reviewers who may quote brief passages in a review.

Book design by Saqib_arshad

Printed in the United States of America

Contents

Introduction	1
Acknowledgement	2
Absent Father	3
A Father's Love	4
Suicide	5
I'm the Problem	6
Introduction to Charles: 101	6
Lisa Ann	7
First Love	8
Keishawna	9
Rhapsody	10
Last Mile	11
Miscarriage	12
Just a Friend	13
Digital Love	14
Mom's Love	15
Momma Love Me	16
Jay	17
Woman	18
Woman II	19
Divine Black Queen	20
Stop Running	21
The Gift of Individuality	23
To This Day!	24
Freedom	25

Foot Prints	26
You	27
Penny Proud	28
I'm Tired of Being a Poet	29
Dad's Inspiration	30
18	31
Happy Birthday	32

Introduction

Divine Charles, also known as The Divine Wordsmith is a Poet, activist, feminist and motivational speaker from Queens, NewYork who is now based in Florida. The wordsmith began saturating a variety of social media platforms such as : Instagram, Facebook and TikTok, in 2018. Charles initially started reciting his late grandmother's poetry at the age of 10 at United Apostolic Church. He later began writing on his own and began performing in various places like school, church and even on the train. He has hosted a number of events in schools as well as open mic venues in Queens and Long Island for the sole purpose of giving artists a space to express themselves and showcase their talents.

Messages From a Boy with an Absentee Father is an anthology about a boy who is transforming into a man without the guidance of a father. The absence of his father creates obstacles on his journey as well as cripples every aspect of his love life. The experiences of the poet alters his perception of how he sees the world, his companions and even himself.

Acknowledgement

If you are reading this right now, thank you for being a Divine supporter. I would like to thank my mother, Claudia for being the super mom that you are and supporting me in all that I do. I would also like to extend a special thanks to my late grandmother, Sonia who was the first person to encourage me to write poetry and recite it in front of an audience. Thank you to my 5 aunts and 2 uncles and who helped raise me (Nadeen, Sophia, Tiffany, Latoya, Sandrene, Omar and Kert). I love you all dearly.

    I am humbled and grateful to share my anthology with all of my friends and family. I must admit that this book would not exist without the love and encouragement of my mentors and teachers. I would like to extend my gratitude to my best friends Anaiya, Ashley P, Ashley S, Maya, and Isaiah; Along with my mentors: Bishop Michael Edwards, Pastor Charles Barrett, Herveriel Gray, Frederick Salomon, Robin Williams, Chris Jacob, Carla Boxcell, Natalie Francois, Kyra Etheridge, Kimberly Mitchel, Natassia Ferguson and Antonette Jones. All of you forced me to stop limiting myself within my craft. I am nothing without this side of the family.

Absent Father

Absent father, where have you gone?
Absent father, tell me what went wrong.
Absent father, i hate to see you fall,
But did you make the effort to pick up the phone and call?
The boy I am today, will shape the man of tomorrow.
The pain of your absence has brought me great sorrow.
Aren't you worried about what I am now?
What will I be?
I'm stuck here, my mind's been brought into captivity.
I need to be emancipated, can't you see?
They say, "The apple doesn't fall too far from the tree".
But I am a promise, not a possibility.
Just wanted you to be by my side to tell me everything's gonna be alright.
I'm on this battlefield, but I don't know how to fight.
Everyone has their fight and we all have to take a stand.
But why can't a father hold his own son's hand?
I wanted you too come back, but why bother.
This is a message from a boy with an absentee father.

- DIVINE WORDSMITH

A Father's Love

Father's are one of God's greatest creations.
Don't believe it?
It's so true.
How do we repay you for the things that you do?
Their obstinance, radiance are second to none.
Our sole protectors since time began.
How do you move a mountain?
How can you drown an ocean?
For His children, he puts these impossible tasks in motion.
He is humble, resilient when the family feels weak.
When the future is blurry, Still, he is faithful and meek.
It isn't an understandable love.
It's the love that dwells in him from above.
A mother's warmth and embrace is indeed sweet.
But, without a father in the front, the family is incomplete.

- DIVINE WORDSMITH

Suicide

They curse at me, and tell me I shouldn't be swearing.
No one listens to my voice, it seems they're only hearing.
It's never easy growing up with a single parent.
I'm depressed and they ignore it though it is apparent.
Saw my close friend who commit suicide on the news.
I'm traumatized,
Flashes of my dad and me being abused.
I try to write to feel better, or suppress the pain.
But everything feels the same.
Sounds of my pen aren't loud enough to overshadow the rain.
I want to end it all and cut the circulation from my veins.
But here, I remain.
I could see the tear in my mother's eye.
All the times she asked if I'm okay and I told her a lie.
The ones who cared would be disappointed by the way that I died.
Not to mention, me leaving my baby sister behind.
So when you feel you've had enough and you wanna go in a hearse,
Think of people you'll leave hurting behind first.

- DIVINE WORDSMITH

I'm the Problem

I'm not the type of man women want to love.
Picture me tryna impress an empress acting like a "thug".
Not gonna happen
Cause in this social media Era everybody wanna be everything except themselves Thinking if they conform to this norm, it'll help.
Oh snap I ain't got no filter
1 outta 3 girls that I've met never learned how to cook.
The other 2 thirds facetime more than they face books.
Not me
Like Hov said I never change cause really, I'm a vibe.
Charming, handsome.
Damn ….double homicide.
But why should I try to abide by the nature of my timeline Maybe I'm behind or they just won't try to understand my mind.
But I got no time for the birds.
And you can save all the slurs.
I crave intimacy
But can only foreplay with these words.
I'm tired
Of seeing an outlet to infatuation
Then I gotta hit the kill switch on every woman I deal with.
Maybe I should be average in order to attain real love.
Be average you know, like a report card 80 and above.
Nowadays it seems nobody understands where I'm coming from.
I think it's time to face the truth, that maybe I'm the problem.

- DIVINE WORDSMITH

Introduction to Charles: 101

Good morning student.
Not that you pay attention.
But I had enough, now class is in session.
This school allowed you to infiltrate and taint this fool.
This school hid its heart in a desk, you have yet to find his jewel.
This school marked you present in your absence.
'Cause it needed your company.
Hoping someday you'd finally show up for me.
This school suspended you time after time.
And still let you off the hook.
Let you read through its pages and vandalize its books.
Well this school is shutting down.
Thought I should let you know.
It's after hours, the principles left a long time ago.
I've had other students, but never like this.
I chaperoned you myself and took you on all my trips.
And still you don't see me.
My only student and I'm still tongue tied.
I'm being looked in the eye by my 1 alumni.
I search within myself to let you go.
You should know.
I don't wanna feel compelled Don't wanna be dragged to Hell.
This school ain't shutting down Baby.
You're getting expelled.

- DIVINE WORDSMITH

Lisa Ann

No one has been there for me.
And I've always had to hold my own.
Since you stepped into my life I don't feel all alone.
You know I always watch over you like a chaperone.
Call me krazy,
But I hope ya uber app crashes just so I can drop you home.
See the truth is really easy to tell,
But harder to express to the one girl that knows you best.
I never wanna leave you and I've never been so sure.
Outta 5 girls I took 3L and 1 W, but no more.
'Cause baby you're, my hero I've called on each time, without a cape.
I never had to question who could I run to, when my mind needed an escape.
And only you would understand
How hard it is to express as a man. But I just wanted you to know I Love you Lisa Ann.

- DIVINE WORDSMITH

First Love

Hello, my love.
Can't recall the last time my pen caressed your papers.
Or when I last enjoyed that new page smell I used savor.
I used to sit alone and cry.
It would be you to dry my eyes.
Only you saw the transparency beneath my lies.
I fell in love with this new way to form letters. Metaphors kissed your papers, Similes became jealous.
Letters became words.
Words became life.
Work became toil and toil begat strife.
But through all my sorrow, you taught me to fight.
Quenching my thirst, satisfying my appetite.
Only you stood by me in my hour of tribulation.
Like butter we melt into an abyss of infatuation
To tell the truth, there's a ton of things I want to say to you.
You were there for me
On the coldest of nights
And
From the first day I was introduced
To
Your spoken words
We loved in metaphor.
For you I'd die for
Put no man above
I will ever embrace your wisdom
You're my first Love

— DIVINE WORDSMITH

Keishawna

From the first day I met you, our eyes made four.
The more I denied it, I wanted you more.
From the first conversation I knew it was meant to be.
Call it blind love,
But that day I carried home your strong perfume scent on my glove.
It's a mystery why we're not together now.
It's been a journey indeed.
Constantly disputing our wants and our needs.
Drooling on the phone, fighting the sleep we lack.
Hang up by accident, then just call right back. Now all I can do is reminisce, On those lips I used to kiss.
Not to mention that smile I'll always miss.
And so I took this time,
To give you a piece of my mind. You can erase me from your mind, But you'll always be mine.

— DIVINE WORDSMITH

Rhapsody

Remember when I asked you to be mine and you said you had to go?
When it didn't work I thought you'd say,"I told you so".
Remember when you fell for me?
You dived and drowned in my love Rhapsodies.
I've wept countless nights, with your pictures in my frame.
Speeding through my contacts to avoid seeing your name.
Some days I weep and lock myself in my room,
And others I smile so blissfully thinking of our honeymoon.
It was just a phase....
We shined brighter in those days
We couldn't predict in a million yrs that we'd be in one another's way.
But it became harder as time passed.
Our blues skies and sunshine blinded us from the real forecast.
Now, who do I wake up and argue with relentlessly?
How was I to know you were sick of me?
I swore, you forget about the last fight in my mind.
Never guess that I'd be unforgiven this time.
I can humbly say that I'm sorry for my demeanor.
But I'm sure that on the other side, the grass doesn't get any greener.

- DIVINE WORDSMITH

Last Mile

Come follow me my love, while the moon is bright.
We can gaze upon the stars of this blurry night.
Come follow me my love.
Let us lay upon the sand.
Make the grooves of the rocks caress each other's hands.
I see the pain in your eyes, though tears are restrained.
You gave him your heart and he took it in vain.
Here I lay to deliver you from a treatment so vile.
Oh rest your feet my love, you've walked your last mile.
When we were just friends, I hated to see you cry.
God predestined this love before you caught my eye.
Ole transparent smile, I see a life filled with gloom.
Day after day, you stayed locked in your room. You've been through enough,
Rest your feet child.
Get comfortable my love, you've walked your last mile.

- DIVINE WORDSMITH

Miscarriage

Sleeping pills and ibuprofen.
My sobriety has been broken.
Weighed on me were the pressures from a man.
Ya know, when your husband expects and all he could do is hold your hand. I'm thinking selfishly like, "When this is over I'll be even fatter." Or, "Can 9 months come any faster, he's on my bladder".
I am selfish!
Though I complained about the pain,
I envisioned the kicks of his soft feet.
My face on his bare chest hearing his heartbeat.
That was the real loss.
I wanted to die with my son.
My husband cries while I hide.
He seeks refuge from me I can't be strong all the time!
I tried to take my life.
Then I realized, we both died that night.
My nightmare followed me home
Things became worse for me
Peeking into that little room with an empty nursery. Baby shower gift perfectly aligned, It just wasn't fair.
A body producing milk for a baby that wasn't even there.
Can I tell my husband I killed our son
That my sobriety was broken for a few hours of fun. No! It would kill him. But after all he knows, I am an addict.

- DIVINE WORDSMITH

Just a Friend

Across the room I hold my gaze.
I saw your smile, I was so amazed.
Why did it take so long for me to see?
You're the only perfect one for me.
You're far away but I need you now.
I want to love you, just show me how.
The closer we get, my emotions run wild.
Tongue tied, looking in your eyes.
Why'd it go?
Fade away.
Why'd it die, why'd it turn to gray?
'Cause I'm falling for you.
It's been a long time, I kept this love rhapsody for you girl.
It seems I was never on time to join the split between our worlds.
Day by day, our romance continues to bend.
Awoken to the oppression of you being just a friend.
Like the grin God gave when he first crafted a star.
So does the sun smile on us, at the horizon afar.
Our progressive relationship continues, like eagles we sore.
Blind loves weep, our eyes make four.
Fractured emotions, scattered pieces won't mend.
Awaken to the oppression of you being just a friend.

- DIVINE WORDSMITH

Digital Love

Our Love, so digital.
Keeping the spark in our relationship alive.
Who knows why I couldn't do it with such a hard drive.
We lost control, you walked away.
I wanted you backSpace …. Wasn't the key.
Less time on the phone was your delete button for me.
Didn't feel real in my mind, Enough time to I- message, No face to facetime.
But I hurt you, you hurt me.
But wait ….
You cut me open.
And where were my stitches?
I'm off track in thinking that this Mac can't get viruses ….
But when we kissed, it made my world spin.
You've changed,
It's a shame, we shutdown.
'Cause you were never logged in.

— DIVINE WORDSMITH

Mom's Love

I appreciated all the things she did.
Every good report card was a trip to Lids.
After every bad one was confinement in my room.
My only friends were my books, the dust and a broom.
The rod was never a spoiler,
It was a conditioner of the mind.
To think of the mistakes I've made over time.
New B's with the Nudies, I owe her much more than diamonds and rubies.
Miles and miles away, I still hear her voice.
Saying, "Make the right choice".
Oblivious to my wrongs, she picked me up when I fell.
Her love is something she's never failed to release.
Without her guidance, there's only a fragment of peace.
Her wisdom she passes on, I can never be alone.
She is my strength and inspiration.
Her heart I've made my home.

- DIVINE WORDSMITH

Momma Love Me

Momma loved me
Grandma kept
Pop neglected me
Tina always respected me
Aj hit me made me tougher
Born as cousins but know you really my brother
Omar raised me
Grandpa embraced me
As a man, he always lended a hand
Nae Nae pushed me to take some chances
Tiff was a party and taught me all of my dances
Sophie funded gave that Honda
They all my aunties but love me like momma
Toya encouraged me to push my pen
Thanking God I never had writer's block again.
Salomon molded me therapy sessions
Friends embraced me had struggles in acceptance.
Pop i forgive you never thought I'd lived to
But your absence is minimal to the things that I've been through.
Shout to Tiwu Shout to 4a.
Lyricism rebirthing the culture in broad day.
God has always been good to me, made ways outta no way.
Miracles sound like a joke to the man that don't pray

- DIVINE WORDSMITH

Jay

"Since I'm in the position to talk to these kids and they listen I ain't a politician but I kick it with em a minute".
For 18 yrs I've been hearing Em killed Hov.
When are yall gonna stop speaking in vain?
Knowing Jay pushed his pen passed his pain.
Bringing the sound of the streets back.
Not tryna be shady, but i think it's type Shady to say he murdered him on his own track. Something about, "I had to hustle my back to the wall, ashy knuckles." Hit different from the way the media sees you.
Your feelings are what you got to harness.
They treat us poets like pigs, we get dragged through the mud regardless.
Then we say the wrong thing and our names get tarnished.
But Jay gave us black men the blueprint to stay out the hood.
I pray that I stay out for good.
Promoting coming up from the hard knock life.
In my lifetime, this is what I'd like to see.
For us kings to realize we belong to a dynasty.
For some of us he was the only role model when TV dad was all we had. Tell us the reality of how they kill us in our house Shoot us in our car 'cause of reasonable doubt.
I learned alot from Jay
Taught me to fend on streets on my own. There may never be another to sit in that spot But at least still get to watch the throne.

- DIVINE WORDSMITH

Woman

The most important thing to give a woman is respect.
And that's the part we forget.
Instead we treat them like the lower beings.
That's how we associate.
Disrespecting the main source for how we procreate.
And men always wanna talk about Eve and her mistakes.
When will she be forgiven?
Some of the greatest civilizations flourished through the ruling of women.
Way back, when Pharaoh died back home.
Queen Hasheput ascended her throne and ruled it all alone.
She was nothing like the kings who dressed in their linen.
She built the first mosque in Africa to educate our women.
Queen Nefertiti, her strut was strong and unapologetic.
She illuminated beauty and discovered cosmetics.
Despised throughout history 'cause she wasn't a man pleaser.
But tell me, without Cleopatra, who was Caesar?
We gotta start treating Queens right.
The gender that made us great.
And realize without our rib, we can't stand up straight. There was a time where they had no rights at all, Let's not create a sequel.
Cut the chains off those doors and make my black women equal.

— DIVINE WORDSMITH

Woman II

Behind every man is a good woman.
Nah she should be in the front.
You treat her like your ashtray, but she's the light to your blunt.
And I'm just being blunt.
Behind every man is absolutely nothing!
Just look into her eye
You're dressing for work while she's tying your tie.
Let me see your smile Queen.
You ain't insecure, just confused and it's clear.
You can embrace your face, but why are you still perming your hair?
My Queens were created in beauty and light.
God is my witness.
The way you strut down every aisle with your crown in its thickness.
Never needed a man either, you just wanna add 'em.
The finest ruby found on Earth formed from an atom.
You're blessed beyond measures or anything you could fathom.
The greatest gift,
Exactly why God gave you to Adam.

- DIVINE WORDSMITH

Divine Black Queen

Dear black Queen,
You are more than they make you out to be.
It's a shame, you wear the heaviest shackles, but deserve to be free.
You fight on the front line.
I think most would agree
Defiled by many forces Which might even include me.
They always stress the power of men.
Like he's some bold figure.
But he can't possess the strength it takes to carry and deliver.
Can she move that mountain?
Are you kidding me?
Resilience?
She is the epitome.
Engraved in my heart, my Queen is immortal.
You make me smile anytime the trials of life trigger me.
Black woman, I love you more than all the riches I can obtain.
They try to knock you out of history,
But like the obstinate rose, still you remain...
Black Queen, you are my rock and the reason I sing.
Thank you for being who you are, and raising a king.

– DIVINE WORDSMITH

Stop Running

From the bushes of Ethiopia To the 13 colonies?
Excuse me for acknowledging this robbery, but this bothers me.
Yeah, they talk about the civil war and how the blacks won.
But never tell us how it started back in 1441.
It was Portugal…
To Africa, that's where the ship went
Prince Henry II needed more gold so that's where they were sent.
Our men had spears, they had cartridges.
They felt fear, we had confidence.
We were Kings, Queens.
It's a shame this is the part of Our history that tarnishes.
We were free on our land and never had to fight to live.
Now my black women and men are statues of incompetence?
No!
Our woman were tough, Men were fervent.
Once free, turned indentured servant.
A brave black man ran away.
Declared he wasn't here to stay.
Serving a man of no color to survive day to day.
Found in Maryland very shortly.
Indentured servants turned slaves in 1640.
We had Tubman, Douglas.
We owe a whole bunch.
But the one they never reveal is the first slave, John Punch.
Black men walking out on their families.
Young children gain Wisdom.
We've been practicing to walk out on our loved ones since the stud system.
Been running my whole life,

Frankly, my spiritual ankles are sore.
So many suffered for centuries, so we wouldn't have to run anymore.

— DIVINE WORDSMITH

The Gift of Individuality

God has given us the gift that we take for granted each day.
The gift we so often use and arrogantly display.
The gift of I.
Symbolic to one's individuality. Essential to the soul as undefined gravity,
Pulling its mass preserving humanity.
Untitled philosophy.
Dominion regulates unconscious territory.
The tongue infiltrates a world of insecurities.
Tearing brothers and sisters down.
Stuck in a world where cries are heard most, but laughter is silence.
Standing on the promises of this world alone.
Piercing the flesh of our very own.
But there's an infinite spirit, the master awaits.
We stand on the promises of our guardians gate.

— DIVINE WORDSMITH

To This Day!

To this day,, As black folks we've learned to evolve
And on you it weighs heavy
Exactly why you try to break us down like a levy.
To this day I'm a slave, this ain't up for no debate.
I can't breathe cause I'm always being stifled by your hate.
To this day it ain't just about hatred, its envy.
You can pretend but we can see
Sitting in the sun tryna tan ya skin.
Sorry not sorry, you'll never match my melanin.
To this day, jealousy is a hard pill to swallow.
Like a virus tryna, overtake a host.
To this day, I ain't never resisted an arrest and you are still doing the most.
To this day you're mad cause you can't have what we got.
I mean you ran through our villages, took the resources too.
Used ya weapons when you realized we can overpower you. To this day, I made you rich 400 and I'm still your b-.
Excuse my French, just tryna make it clear.
My ancestors are the reason you're flourishing here.
To this day, I put my hands in the air, you shoot at me.
To this day, you Humiliate me on camera for the world to see.
We try to uproot forces of racism, and you just plant a bigger tree.
To this day, they cover our eyes so we can't see.
To this day, I am a promise and not a possibility.

- DIVINE WORDSMITH

Freedom

My freedom, to me, is living inside of my head.
Knowing the opposition thinks I'm better off dead.
My freedom doesn't actually exist here.
Since I'm shot at when I clearly have my hands in the air.
My freedom is the way my pen strokes across these pages.
Since speaking up wasn't enough, you've been muting us for ages.
I mean, take a look at me.
Naked, stripped of my dignity, Clothed in depravity.
You got my people in fear.
Streets saturated with black grieving mothers' tears.
You rather shoot us down in cold blood, then show love.
Don't you dare mute the words of my lips when our bodies have become safe havens for hollow tips.
So when you ask me what is freedom
My response to you is, how the Hell should I know?
When I was born with these chains.
Shirts stick to my back pasted with blood stains.
You try to wipe us out of history and burned our remains
Enslaved by race, when the same color runs in our veins.
So my emancipation is me riding my bike without feeling alarmed.
Walking down the street without being shot unarmed.
Sean Bell, Sean Reid, Mr. Arbery, Breonna Taylor.
These spirits cry out for vengeance.
How bout a guilty white man endure the full ride of a sentence.
Or just one black baby delivered without being defiled upon entrance.
'Cause we're not born with freedom.
It's something we've gotta find.
And our only way through is to manifest it as a state of mind.

— DIVINE WORDSMITH

Foot Prints

My greatest fear is to leave this world without my footprints in the sand.
For generations to arrive and be oblivious to the labors of my hands.
Not for acknowledgement or any special recognition, but for my kin to develop a sense of ambition.
To change the world …
To seek God
And one day, into his eyes we will gaze.
Rolling sounds of praise to bring us through our days.
And loathing the virtues in mankind's wicked ways.
I do have faith
We'll unite some day
Where our master once forbid,
He will take the grief of man and mend the weeping rib.

- DIVINE WORDSMITH

You

Listen!
You really need to control yourself and the things you do.
Everything that drags me down traces back to you.
And god of course.
But you don't even pray anymore.
You say you're a Christian with one foot out the door.
You :gotta rubber laugh and a plastic smile.
I haven't seen a genuine reflection in a while.
You try to outsmart God, it isn't good for your health
Knowing he knows you more than you know yourself. You let em push you around take you for the clown You sit back and pretend.
So Desperate to keep a friend.
You're not the same man and you know that it's true.
When they stop accepting you, you'll just move on to something new.
And still, flattered by the barren, "I love you".
You spent all this time trying to free your mind.
Not realizing God's gift was to love and be kind.

— DIVINE WORDSMITH

Penny Proud

I knew God was an artist when he sculpted me.
God who doesn't see race, but if life was about a race.
I'd come in 3rd each and every time.
And through the hollow celebration of the silver and gold medalists
I'd embrace in the mirror a haze of beautiful bronze.
I'd rather be copper colored. Even though it hurts to be.
My grandmother told me,
"If you don't learn to pick up pennies you will never have money".
The question is why
Why
Am I defiled,
Swept like onto the subway
Hoping, someone would look down, and say that it's their lucky day.
But they say
Pressure makes diamonds
Well I require pressure too
I would rather be copper colored 'cause you wouldn't see right through me.
Being black has always been an unsolved mystery.
Not fear or evil, but the color of vitality.
So when you finish in third place celebrate and thank God for gracing you with such a vibrant color.
Until then my kin will sing of these hymns.
And know that they are more precious than a gem.
And hopefully, someday the world may not look down and not step over them.

— DIVINE WORDSMITH

I'm Tired of Being a Poet

I'm tired of being a poet.
Sometimes I'm not okay and I never seem to show it.
Tired of sharing my opinion, people saying they're worthless.
Laughed at just cause I see beyond the surface.
Well I'm sorry I pick your brain and leave you hung.
Or that women love me, just for the swiftness of my tongue.
I'm tired of being a poet.
The clechés, "You're so talented".
No babygirl, you love Divine.
But can you handle Christopher Deevan Charles, sister? You applaud and snap with your purse in your lap, 'Til your thumbs blister.
Can you accept me, without sweet words rolling off my tongue, your ears enchanted, centered stage with your camera slanted?
No one cares how I feel.
All they care for is the sex appeal and whatever's real. And you dare chant, recite another, But I can never heal.
Open mic?
It's more like my open heart.
You applaud my trauma while I'm torn apart.
I'm tired of being a poet.
But you already know I'll never stop.
This pen never neglected me.
I make you smile, make you cry.
'Cause this is who I'm meant to be.

                                         - DIVINE WORDSMITH

Dad's Inspiration

As a young boy, my father wasn't always around.
When he was, I gave pathetic stares at him in his failed attempts to beat my mother to the ground.
The burden stayed on my heart, seeing him spit in my eye.
The only time I gasped for air was when I cried.
He swept us away like dust on a broom.
Flames of tears with a heart consumed.
I've been watching him to see if he'd appear on the news.
For him to get 25 to life something much more than a bruise. I don't know what was worse, Physical or verbal abuse.
Or when he came back apologizing with an excuse.
About the things he had,
About his dad,
But at least he was there for him, he should be glad.
I don't need him.
No tears left in my eyes.
No exception, it's too late for him to apologize.

- DIVINE WORDSMITH

18

This poem is in no way used to amuse.
This is for you young black man who watched his mother get abused.
Let me warn you you'll never get over it.
And I don't mean to be a pessimist but you'll be making up for your "Pops" leaving you in deficit.
But He'll get his Cause you only profit off of what you put in.
So It aint your fault.
Mom became the pawn.
And on account of him the love was overdrawn.
You watched verbal abuse become physical.
The only thing they agree on is that you're the residual.
It was supposed to be 3 of you other women got in between.
Can't believe Momma signed up for this Pyramid scheme.
'Cause he's a fraud !
Exactly why you gotta be somebody, get somewhere Success is a must.
She confides in you and you're a part of her trust.
I know you don't hate your pops cause you help him as a man.
Never ask for repayment.
God Saw the deeds and put it all in your statements.
What I will say to you is, don't let him leave you bankrupt.
Invest in yourself.
Preserve your soul.
That's the difference between riches and wealth.

- DIVINE WORDSMITH

Happy Birthday

Dear Dad,

Happy birthday.
It's your second son.
Ya know the one born on Christmas Day.
That you call when you need something, then throw it away.
I thought of calling you, I hesitated in between.
Seeing how you've missed a couple of my birthdays since I was 13.
But my grandmother said never render evil for evil.
So I wish you growth and prosperity.
But I thought I'd tell you, I forgive you.
For all the traumas I faced as a child.
I mean compared to what I could've been I came out pretty mild.
No one was there to teach me how to be a man as a kid So I resorted to doing the opposite of what you did.
It backfired.
It felt like being in prison, tryna be a good man Still taken for granted by women.
I can't blame you anymore, I had to find a balance.
Dating, not knowing how to treat a woman was a challenge.
Gotta admit, I'm grateful for the push you gave me. And I can assure you, over here, you have no grand babies My sister is fine, but I must confess.
When you tell me to tell her hello, I choose not to ruin her day.
Giving hope for a relationship with you, just to snatch it away.
Cause you're too inconsistent.
At one point you were my favorite artist. Then you became a zero.
You didn't even know
Before I even had an imagination my dad was my hero.

And just in case you feel like it's little Chris thinking about you with tears in his eyes. I'm a poet and a grown ass man now, this is merely a lyrical exercise.

Sincerely,
The second bastard.

www.ingramcontent.com/pod-product-compliance
Lightning Source LLC
Chambersburg PA
CBHW042306150426
43197CB00001B/32